National Institute of Justice

Stalking Research Workshop
Meeting Summary

June 17, 2010

Crystal Gateway Marriott
Arlington, Virginia

Table of Contents

Welcome, Opening Comments, Facilitator Introductory Remarks and Overview

Bernie Auchter, Acting Division Director, National Institute of Justice

Mr. Auchter opened the meeting and introduced National Institute of Justice (NIJ) Acting Director Kristina Rose.

Kristina Rose, Acting Director, National Institute of Justice

Ms. Rose explained that NIJ wants to develop comprehensive, on-the-mark research agendas and thus sought input and expertise from people at this meeting. She noted that domestic violence, sexual assault and stalking are all recognized as crimes of violence against women and that stalking is often a significant component of intimate partner violence. The dynamics around stalking are constantly in flux, she added, with changing technology such as instant messaging and texting, and so what is reported now may not be relevant in a year or two. But, as technology used to stalk improves, so does technology to find, prosecute and convict stalkers. Some prosecutors understand the crime, and some have become specialists. She expressed NIJ's excitement about the participation of meeting attendees as they worked to generate and prioritize a research agenda focused on the prevention of and responses to stalking.

Thanks to the Violence Against Women Act, Ms. Rose said, NIJ has been fortunate to have a dedicated funding stream to research violence against women, and significantly more money has been budgeted for next year. The Office on Violence Against Women (OVW) has been a strong partner in supporting NIJ's research portfolio. NIJ has also worked in the past with the Bureau of Justice Statistics (BJS) on the stalking supplement to the National Crime Victimization Survey. NIJ wants to continue work with BJS to draft additional supplements, Ms. Rose added. Regardless of our efforts, she concluded, we want to be sure we are covering the right things and asking the right questions when researching stalking; i.e., measuring effectiveness of protection and interventions.

Marnie Shiels [for Susan Carbon, Director], Attorney Advisor, Office on Violence Against Women

Ms. Shiels informed meeting attendees that OVW has been funding the Stalking Resource Center, part of the National Center for Victims of Crime, since 2000. The Stalking Resource Center provides training and technical assistance to enhance responses to stalking and is committed to collecting the best knowledge about stalking, including researching policy and tracking program success.

Bethany Backes, Social Science Analyst, National Institute of Justice

Ms. Backes described the format for today's meeting, reviewed the agenda and invited people at the table to introduce themselves. She also reviewed the handouts provided to participants prior to the meeting that included a discussion question guide, BJS's *Special Report: Stalking Victimization in the United States* and *Stalking Policies and Research in the United States: A Twenty-Year Retrospective.*

Research on Partner Stalking: Putting the Pieces Together
T.K. Logan, Professor, University of Kentucky

Dr. Logan summarized findings related to intimate partner stalking research. More information about the findings is available at http://www.ncvc.org/src/AGP.Net/Components/DocumentViewer/Download.aspxnz?DocumentID=48094.

Generally, Dr. Logan noted, intimate partner stalking is the largest category of stalking. Studies have shown that incidence ranges from 4.8 to 14.5 percent for women versus 0.6 percent of men. She said that rates of partner stalking among college women are high (5.3 percent in a period of approximately seven months). Those stalked by an ex-partner likely experienced partner violence and sexual assault during the relationship with that partner. Further, studies of women with histories of partner violence who were also stalked by the violent partner suggest that 80 to 90 percent were stalked during the relationship. However, stalking during periods of separation is common, and the intensity and frequency tend to increase during these periods. Stalking victims reported more separation attempts than victims of partner violence who were not stalked. After obtaining a protective order, stalking victims were less likely to return to the relationship with the violent partner than were non-stalked victims of partner violence. Being stalked during periods of separation poses significant risk.

Dr. Logan said that stalkers use a variety of tactics. The most frequent tactic is physical surveillance (watching, spying on, following, waiting for the victim or showing up in places where the stalker knows the victim may be). Other stalking tactics include unwanted phone calls, letters, gifts, e-mails, text messages or property invasion. Alternatively, other people may take part in the stalking; i.e., proxy stalking. Technology widens the arsenal of tactics, she said, with 26.5 percent of stalking victims reporting cyber-stalking or electronic monitoring.

Intimate partner stalkers (versus acquaintance and stranger stalkers) tend to be more violent, insulting and persistent (2.2 years of stalking by former intimate partners versus 1.1 years of stalking by non-intimate partners); more likely to escalate in frequency and intensity of pursuit; and more likely to use more tactics. Partner stalkers are also more likely to reoffend after a court order and to do so more quickly than non-intimate partner stalkers.

Dr. Logan added that stalking is associated with femicide or attempted femicide (90 percent of women who were murdered or against whom murder attempts were made were stalked). Not all offenders who commit partner violence also stalk their victims; the research shows that about half do. Of those who do stalk their partner or ex-partner, victims report more severe physical abuse, sexual abuse and control.

Stalking is also associated, Dr. Logan noted, with protective order violations. Several studies found that about half of the women who sought protective orders were stalked the year before they obtained the order. Although 61 to 65 percent of stalkers desist after the protective order, about a third of them persist in stalking and abuse.

Dr. Logan said that the collateral impact, in addition to fear and distress, includes impaired health and financial strain and detrimental effects on children, friends, family members and social life. She added that fear causes multidimensional effects, such as significant depression, anxiety, post-traumatic stress, pain, and sleep and health disorders. There also appears to be a dose/response relationship, with more frequent or intense stalking associated with greater negative impact on the victim's life. Employed women are subjected to a greater number of tactics and stalking that lasts three times longer than stalking of unemployed women. Women who have experienced stalking by an intimate partner lose professional opportunities because of job interference caused by harassment, disruption or performance problems (e.g., trouble concentrating). Stalking victims also experience significantly more property damage than victims who were never stalked or who were stalked before but not after the protective order. Financial costs incurred, Dr. Logan noted, include credit problems, identity theft, safety measures, legal fees, and health and mental health treatment. Children are used as tools, targets or allies, and in many cases the children are afraid as well. Partner stalking is also costly to society.

Not all stalking victims report their experiences, Dr. Logan said. Police response may be inadequate because officers do not understand the offense or do not know what to do. For each case identified, an estimated 21 are missed. Charging stalkers helps to hold them accountable, but prosecution and conviction rates are lower than the estimated number of cases or than rates for similar misdemeanor charges.

Discussion of *Research on Partner Stalking: Putting the Pieces Together*

The discussion included the following:

- The crime is definitely under-identified. In the study "The Role of Stalking in Domestic Violence Crime Reports Generated by the Colorado Springs Police Department," Dr. Tjaden and co-author Nancy Thoennes looked for evidence of stalking (whether the victim mentioned it, or the operational description was satisfied) in records of police complaints of domestic violence in Colorado. Out of 1,700 cases, 1 in 6 showed evidence of stalking (repeated actions, fear and invasiveness), and of those 300 cases, only one resulted in an official file. The definition of stalking is problematic. Some studies use a list of items to define stalking.

- Meeting attendees discussed protection order data. Which variable indicates that stalking stopped? Is it the victim's perception that the behavior stopped, or is it the absence of further police reports?

- An early study by the Threat Management Group showed that having a detective follow up on a police report helps deter stalkers. But whether this really works or escalates the problem must be determined case by case. It may depend on the type of stalker — partner versus acquaintance versus stranger — and the history of intimate partner violence.

- In 2006, as part of the National Crime Victimization Survey, the Bureau of Justice Statistics completed the Supplemental Crime Victimization Survey, which used some 300 variables. This study can be sliced many different ways and is publicly available through the National Archive of Criminal Justice Data.

- In November 2010 in Oklahoma, a law will go into effect that permits conviction for stalking without the victim experiencing fear; instead, the law requires that the victim experience "severe emotional distress." Fear is still critical to the definition of stalking and is difficult to measure. The National Violence Against Women Survey used a definition of stalking that involved a high level of fear for the victim. However, when they used a definition of stalking that involved the victim's feeling "somewhat" or "a little" frightened, the statistics changed significantly and included a higher proportion of male victims. If "fear" is replaced by "emotional distress," it may also change the figures dramatically and potentially impact the gender ratio.

Discussion of Research Gaps: Law Enforcement and Prosecution

Using the discussion questions as a guide, participants were asked to discuss research gaps and critical research questions to consider as they relate to law enforcement and prosecution.

Incidence
- Intimate partner stalking accounts for only about a third of offenders. Police Chiefs have said that surveillance technology, such as cameras, outside the victims' homes increases the number of arrests and saves the police department money — and people pay attention to money-saving techniques.

- Law enforcement minimizes stalking, but the crime is important. It takes a lot for a victim to come forward in the first place. Police who deal with this should not think of themselves as a stalking unit, but as a homicide-prevention unit — and that is the kind of thing that can lead to a culture change across law enforcement agencies. At the same time, the most serious cases are a challenge to identify, and identifying those cases could create better police buy-in.

- Victims don't use the word "stalking." There is a general misconception that because stalking is a nonviolent crime, stalkers are not violent. For police to take the offense seriously, stalkers have to behave in ways or say things that indicate that their perceptions do not correspond to reality and that they are likely to become violent.

- Someone should analyze all the reports to find the suicide data. It might reveal places we could have intervened.
- From a research perspective, why are the numbers inconsistent across studies?

Protection orders
- There is a need to understand how victims experience stalking as well as how their needs change over time.
- There is limited information on how protection orders assist stalking victims. When are protection orders necessary, and for what length of time?
- How can the field make protection orders more accessible to stalking victims, as stalking is a difficult crime to prove?

Response
- There is a need for more coordination among divisions and departments within and across law enforcement organizations. Intimate partner violence cases in the District of Columbia are well known in different divisions, but people in one division don't talk to people in other divisions.
- The mismatch between the law and police enforcement makes us wary of using the word "seriousness" because of not wanting to minimize the act; each incident should be treated seriously. Also, the problem is not just that stalkers are not being charged, but that often when they are, the charges are later reduced. Minimization is critical and occurs among victims themselves, so they do not report everything. The police say they can't charge a stalker until something happens because they don't realize that stalking and unwanted contact amount to a crime.
- In Rhode Island, stalking is a felony, but in the field it is not considered a "real" felony. Stalkers may be violent, but are probably more likely to drive the victim to suicide — an area that has not been studied, but should be, because whether the victim is murdered or commits suicide, the end result is preventable loss of life.
- Law enforcement officers don't know how to follow up and get evidence and need better tools and training on how to investigate stalking.
- We need to bring criminal justice together with advocacy, and advocacy together with prosecution. Then, we need boundary-spanning practices to bring the different pieces of the response together.
- Content analyses of police and prosecutorial reports are needed. How is stalking being documented in police reports, and what leads to prosecutorial action?

Arrest
- How do we get the criminal justice system to arrest stalkers? Over time, the number of arrests and charges has increased, but the gap between the law and actual practice and criminal prosecutors is huge. Police make an effort to identify cases, but intake reports should be changed so police are required to routinely ask about stalking in intimate partner violence cases.

- The patrol officer's job is not to investigate. In Minnesota, when officers were required to ask a few additional questions, the stalking statistics rose. However, since stalking is a misdemeanor, the perpetrators are jailed and released if they have $2,800. The Enhancement Project logs each offender's convictions for the last 5 years, so it is easy to see the history on the enhancement sheet. Police officers don't have time to do research, but they are not averse to using the facts at hand.
- The Philadelphia Police Department started a directive, but it must be evaluated to know whether it is a best practice. They also have instituted a palm-card list of questions. This highlights the need for evaluation of the effectiveness of policy implementation, training and the use of palm cards by first responders. Have the various elements they have implemented over the years led to more arrests, more convictions, safer victims, etc.? Did one element have more of a significant effect than another?
- Law enforcement's responsibilities should be expanded to helping victims; e.g., St. Paul uses a danger assessment, but such practices need to be evaluated for their effectiveness.
- Recidivism is twice as high among those not arrested as those arrested.
- Medical and mental health personnel should be better engaged or brought in to conduct screenings.

Gone on arrival
- There is the phenomenon of the suspect being "gone on arrival." Any offender arrested once knows that chances are good that s/he will not be charged if s/he disappears immediately. The first step is to get police to write "gone on arrival" in the report. However, when the offender has fled, a warrant can be requested without the victim's cooperation.
- Getting warrants for those people increases arrest rates. Moreover, they were also found to be more serious offenders than ones who had not left the scene.
- Tangible incidents should be reported that occur within the context of stalking (e.g., running the victim off the road, destroying her property, home invasion).
- Is there a qualitative difference between "gone on arrival" when a no-contact order is in place and when it is not? Officers may suspect there is a no-contact order when the victim says, "He's not supposed to be here."

Community response
- Developing a community response is important, and a countywide protocol would be helpful. Counter-stalking efforts in police departments constitute one way to get such a protocol.
- The issue of community response is not just related to criminal justice, but also community perceptions. We have to overcome the idea that the fastest way for the police to help a woman is to jail the offender.
- We need to raise awareness. We could look at youth and get their views of technology.
- Actions go in concentric circles and overlap around stalking. Maybe we should change our goals. Educating the media is very important because it will educate the community.

- There is a need to examine how the media is using the word stalking and how they are describing stalking situations. Is the media downplaying stalking as a crime?

Jurisdiction
- Stalking across boundaries adds to the complexity of the crime. It is necessary to have better communication across jurisdictions.
- Jurisdictional issues (including interstate) are huge because even e-mails crossing state lines can turn into a federal offense so we also need to know about federal responses.
- How do we get jurisdictions to work together to share information? Many jurisdictions may not have the data systems or infrastructure to support cross-jurisdictional communication.
- Evaluation of smaller jurisdictional responses is needed.

Risk assessment
- Currently, there are no validated stalking-specific risk assessment tools. There are general risk/threat assessment tools and tools related to intimate partner violence that may incorporate elements of stalking, but there is a need for a stalking-specific tool.
- Victims are good at assessing risk themselves. In scenario planning, victims help identify scenarios where violence might occur.
- Risk factors for danger are not monitored. One major area of lost opportunity is the focus of many law enforcement officers on arrest rather than risk assessment. One purpose of risk assessment is to get the victim to understand the seriousness of her/his situation, which should also inform law enforcement of the need to investigate further.
- We need to assess risk of increased violence and find out who the most severe offenders are. Where they enter the system determines their path through it, including the particular officers with whom they end up working.

Training
- Training is overrated, especially as the content of the training may be constantly changing to reflect emerging trends. Departments have no performance standards on stalking arrests, so they do not know whether they are doing a bad or a good job.
- Regardless, some training for law enforcement is key, and we need to know what training programs already exist and if they are helping to improve the criminal justice response to stalking.
- Judges need additional training and should be providing more protective orders. In addition, training must extend to the district attorney's office. We are still trying to educate prosecutors. Often advocates have to explain to prosecutors how to deal with a case in which everything happened by e-mail or cell phone.
- Is there a way to measure the effectiveness of training?
- What types of training are available? Training probation officers on the dynamics of stalking may be a good option.

- Also important to training are the potential generation gaps regarding technology and monitoring.
- Training offers a way to bring about culture shift, but every time you hold a training session, you confront the same kind of arguments. This repetition can become frustrating to advocates.

Culture change
- A culture change is needed, as is extensive training so that police can write reports with comprehensive stalking information and serve as effective witnesses in stalking cases. We need to change the way police are trained to respond to stalking. Also, due to high turnover of law enforcement, it is necessary to have a systematic approach to this training.
- Culture change is needed among other criminal justice professionals as well, including prosecutors and judges.
- Other ways to change culture may include rules changes. Who is at the table is an important factor. We need a qualitative study that involves getting victims to talk about what kinds of strategies work and how prosecution and law enforcement fit into it.
- Another big issue is how judges and others are being held accountable in their jobs. Are they concerned just with the number of successful prosecutions?

Fear standard
- If the fear standard for stalking victims were removed from legislation, this change would lower the threshold for the definition of stalking and widen the pool of people who could be arrested for stalking offenses. In the future we should research what happens when states change the definition of stalking and adopt an "emotional distress" standard. We need to know the impact of changing legislation as it relates to arrest and prosecution.

Stalkers
- Stalking is part of a pattern of behavior, sometimes lasting for years. A full picture has to be developed so that stalking behavior is better understood and not minimized.
- We should evaluate probation and parole management and responses when working with stalkers. There is little to no validated research on behavioral therapy with stalkers and on interventions geared towards stalking offenders.
- The available research has shown that there is minimal effectiveness of psychotherapy or pharmacotherapy on lessening stalking behavior. High-intensity management such as intensive parole or probation supervision needs to be examined further.
- With the advent of technology, stalkers can stalk 24 hours a day, 7 days a week. We need to remember that technology does not create stalkers; however, technology can make it easier to stalk and make victims more accessible to the offender.

Prosecution
- We have to look at criminal justice actions and the prosecution system, which is bifurcated into misdemeanors and felonies. Within criminal justice and prosecution, stalking is not viewed as being as serious as a felony, and is not treated seriously in felony court. Furthermore, stalking cases are time consuming because the behaviors are ongoing, so it may take a lot of time and work to collect evidence and to pull the case together. Also, getting juries and judges to understand the dynamics of stalking is difficult, thus case preparation can take longer. Victims are scared and may be less willing to cooperate or to be available — and, because prosecution does not necessarily protect victims, the stalking may be ongoing through the process.
- Prosecutors charge stalking as a misdemeanor, which frustrates law enforcement — maybe judges would not believe the charges. Meanwhile, juries buy into the social media, which portray stalking as romantic and not a serious problem. Departments that have stalking-specific prosecutors should be studied.
- Law enforcement officers say they arrest stalkers, but prosecutors would not prosecute, so they stopped making the arrests. Is it that reports are not being written in a way that allows prosecutors to make charges? Is it that law enforcement is not collecting enough evidence? What needs to be changed to lead to greater numbers of both arrests and prosecutions?
- There is a huge gap between the law and legislators, and law enforcement and criminal justice. Laws have been written in such a way that the two parties are not coming together to address the issues.
- What factors contribute to prosecutors' decisions about how to prosecute?
- Has the situation improved over the 10 years during which stalking has been a focus? Is there more clarity, specialization and training? We may need to do qualitative research around interventions and key stages in the decision-making process. Why do so many stalking cases get dismissed? We could assess the effect that the lack of prosecution has on the victims. We also need more computer case file review.
- The two biggest barriers to prosecution are victim cooperation and the challenge of convincing a jury.
- Prosecutions are complicated by their political nature. An appropriate measure is arrest and conviction per capita. We have to look at the system of criminal justice over time for officers who play different roles within this system. The system should respond in a manner proportionate to the amount of victimization in the community.

Third-party stalking
- We do not inquire about surveillance by third parties. Does it suggest greater risk? Would third-party intervention make a difference?
- In the appendix of the Bureau of Justice Statistics (BJS) report are results of questions asking about number of offenders — fraternities or other organization members, friends, relatives. A third of stalking instances involve more than one offender.

BJS survey

- BJS surveyed victims about the criminal justice system and law enforcement responses to their stalking victimization. In the next survey, what three questions would you like to have asked for the purpose of getting answers at the national level?

Stalking Victimization in the United States: Findings From the National Crime Victimization Survey
Katrina Baum, Senior Statistician, Bureau of Justice Statistics

Dr. Baum reported that the Bureau of Justice Statistics (BJS) had completed the largest scale study to date on stalking with funding from the Office on Violence Against Women. She explained that funding was provided to supplement the National Crime Victimization Survey to include a 10-minute supplement on stalking victimization.

Dr. Baum said that for the Supplemental Victimization Survey (i.e., stalking survey), more than 65,000 people 18 years and older were interviewed from January to June 2006. Key findings from this study include that an estimated 3.4 million people each year were victims of stalking, and the majority of these victims were female, between 18 and 24 years of age, non-Hispanic, divorced or separated, members of lower income households, and college educated.
Dr. Baum noted that the study focused on behavior and did not use the word "stalking." Stalking may be defined with the lay definition, the federal definition or state statute definitions, which vary in terminology for the standard of fear or emotional distress. She said that this survey classified people as stalking victims if they feared for their own safety or that of a family member as a result of the course of conduct or had experienced additional threatening behaviors that would cause a reasonable person to feel fear.

The stalking screening questions in the supplement addressed seven behaviors: making unwanted phone calls or leaving messages; sending unsolicited and unwanted letters, e-mail, etc.; showing up at places without a legitimate reason; following or spying on the victim; waiting for the victim; leaving unwanted items, presents or flowers; and posting information or spreading rumors about the victim on the Internet, in a public place or by word of mouth. The most prevalent fears, Dr. Baum reported, were that they did not know what would happen next, the behavior would never stop, they would experience bodily harm, their child would be harmed or kidnapped, or another family member would be harmed.

The full report can be accessed at http://bjs.ojp.usdoj.gov/index.cfm?ty=pbdetail&iid=1211 or view and download the PDF version of the report at http://bjs.ojp.usdoj.gov/content/pub/pdf/svus.pdf [PDF - 480 Kb]. The National Crime Victimization Survey is currently undergoing a significant redesign. One of the goals for the redesign is to have a more flexible instrument that could use a core and module model to incorporate supplements on various topics on a more regular basis.

Discussion: *Stalking Victimization in the United States*: Findings From the National Crime Victimization Survey

- Context is important and may determine whether a behavior is called stalking. Although context could not be addressed empirically in this research, the Bureau of Justice Statistics survey includes a variable in that it asked victims what their relationship was to their stalkers. It also addressed context in the narratives that respondents provided. From these narratives, we may be able to obtain additional information about the context of the victim-offender relationship, which in turn may help us to learn more about proxy stalking, which is said to be common but is also known to be difficult to measure.
- The 46 percent who do not consider their experience to be stalking are important. When the police correctly identify stalking, there is a positive correlation with reduction and re-abuse. If the victim is told she is being stalked, it makes a big difference — half of the cure is diagnosing the disease. The 46 percent is a substantial proportion of victims who do not consider themselves to have experienced stalking, and though it makes sense that many people may not realize that they have been victims of this crime, it does not indicate that these people are afraid of saying they are being stalked. Instead, it is the same issue that arises with juries — people in general believe that stalking happens to strangers or celebrities, and so people are less likely to recognize themselves as stalking victims, and juries are less likely to convict the person on trial of the crime.
- The definition of stalking includes the fear factor, and if a woman wants a protective order, she must say she is afraid. Both the legal system and victims use various types of language that can help and harm. There is a gap across the board with violence.
- An important issue to consider is that stalking sometimes limits a victim's mobility.

Discussion: Issues With Measurement and Sampling

Using the discussion questions as a guide, participants were asked to discuss research gaps and critical research questions to consider as related to measurement and sampling.

- Researchers must understand how method affects outcome; e.g., phrasing questions, using male or female interviewers (men are more likely to report victimization to other men). A multiple-definition design allows the researcher to go back and analyze the data using different definitions as the laws change. In this design, researchers start with broad screening questions and then use follow-up questions.
- Protective order violations may indicate stalking behavior, so analyzing them may be a cost-effective way to find cases, but this approach would miss a large number of victims.
- In Kentucky, half of the protective orders were reported violated. These violations involved property damage, explicit threat or perceived threat. Surveyors asked for behaviors as well as perceptions — half reported there were violations; half did not. If stalking results in physical harm, the outcome is very different.

- The Centers for Disease Control and Prevention's National Intimate Partner and Sexual Violence Surveillance System (http://www.cdc.gov/violenceprevention/pub/NISVS.html) is a new annual surveillance system that will be looking at stalking victimization. The goal of the system is to generate accurate prevalence and incidence victimization rates of intimate partner violence, sexual violence, stalking and dating violence.

Definitions

- Definitions are crucial. With intimate partner violence offenders, outcomes change dramatically over time with political context and changing laws. This relates to whether an intervention works. Should we pursue some kind of standard definition in this arena? It would be helpful if in the future we were able to look across many studies.
- For policymaking we need to have a problem in order for resources to be devoted to it. Not having a clear definition makes it difficult to address.
- There would be real utility in creating some definition, e.g., criminal versus civil versus personal versus mental health. These would be definitions evolving with our experience. "Emotional distress" is imperfect, but it gives prosecutors leeway to work. Also, we need to look at different areas of life, not just the criminal justice aspect.
- The national response to stalking differs from the community response. Stalking was first defined by the criminal justice community. No matter what the definition, we have to go back to minimization. We cannot rely on victims' responses after years of abuse. A definition must also encompass articulated fear as well as demonstrated fear.
- Training is connected to the definition question. Whatever definitions come about for research reasons, we have to make sure that they will be translated to field operations.
- People exhibit a range of behaviors, from the behaviors of people who would be considered normal to the behaviors of those that would be considered mentally ill, so we need more than one standard.
- Many problems with identification can be clarified through research.

Fear

- The fear component requires that we focus on the victim's response; the stalker's tactics are personal, so the meaning for the victim has to be present. Also, the role of post-traumatic stress is important to consider, because this type of stress may cause people to be emotionally flat.
- Coercive control and entrapment seem to be key.
- What has not been discussed is the notion that people don't think they are victims and that they are being stalked. There are also marginalized communities who don't report feeling fearful.
- Stalking is part of a larger set of actions, and maybe we should focus on control; e.g., people talk about sexual assault versus coercion ("Have you ever thought about what would happen if you didn't consent to sex?").

Offenders
- Stalking continues even after the offender has been arrested or incarcerated through the telephone, letters or use of a proxy to stalk the victim.

Goals
- In the field, we think about how to make information relevant, but we don't know the best practices to implement.
- What we want to accomplish — stop stalking, keep victims safer — will drive what we do and how we plan meetings. We need more probation officers, correction officials, legislators and judges at meetings like this so they are part of the conversation.

Stalking Policy and Legislative Overview
Patricia Tjaden, Director, Tjaden Research Corporation

Rush to Pass Stalking Laws Is Unprecedented

Dr. Tjaden noted that changes in the law usually occur slowly and unevenly, emerging first in one jurisdiction or geographic region and only gradually moving to another. However, she said, this was not the case with stalking legislation. Before 1990, there were no laws in the country that outlawed stalking. Three years later, several states had passed some type of law criminalizing stalking.

1993 Model Anti-Stalking Code

Dr. Tjaden said that, because Congress was concerned that the rush to pass stalking statutes was creating a hodgepodge of flawed and unenforceable laws, in 1992 it charged the National Institute of Justice (NIJ) with development of a model anti-stalking code for states that would be both constitutional and enforceable. NIJ contracted with the National Criminal Justice Association to develop the Code, which was presented to Congress in 1993.

Acknowledging that stalkers can be extremely creative in their methods, the 1993 Model Anti-Stalking Code recommends that states define stalking as "a course of conduct that would cause a reasonable person fear" rather than listing specific stalking behaviors. It further defines the course of conduct as "repeatedly maintaining physical proximity." The 1993 Model Anti-Stalking Code does not require a "credible threat" because it recognizes that stalkers do not always threaten their victims verbally or in writing but instead engage in conduct which, taken in context, would cause a reasonable person fear. Because stalking statutes criminalize what would otherwise be legitimate behavior based upon the fact that the behavior induces fear, the 1993 Model Anti-Stalking Code recommends that stalking statutes include a high standard of fear — fear of bodily injury or death — to the victim or a member of the victim's immediate family.

Stressing the seriousness of the crime, the 1993 Model Anti-Stalking Code recommends that stalking be classified as a felony.

2007 Model Stalking Code

In 2007, Dr. Tjaden said, the National Center for Victims of Crime, under a grant from NIJ, revised the original Model Anti-Stalking Code for states to bring it in line with research findings and the emergence of new tracking and monitoring technologies. The revised 2007 Model Stalking Code, she related, recommends that stalking laws include a legislative intent section that acknowledges the seriousness of the crime and the need for police intervention. It also recommends that state statutes define course of conduct broadly enough to include new technologies and to acknowledge that stalking behavior may be idiosyncratic and thus unique to the victim. Given new tracking and monitoring technologies that allow stalkers to terrorize their victims without ever coming into contact with them, it recommends that stalking statutes no longer define stalking as "repeatedly maintaining physical proximity."

The 2007 Model Stalking Code adopts a general-intent approach, meaning the state need to prove only that the stalker intended to commit his/her actions, not that he/she intended to cause the victim fear. It also recommends that stalking statutes use a reasonable-person standard of fear rather than requiring the victim to feel actual fear. The 2007 Model Stalking Code broadens the level of fear requirement to include emotional distress. It also expands the level and standard of fear requirements to include third parties. Like the original 2003 Model Anti-Stalking Code, the 2007 Code recommends classifying stalking as a felony.

State Stalking Statutes Continue to Vary Widely

Dr. Tjaden reported that although some states have modified their original stalking statutes to conform to recommendations in both the 1993 Model Anti-Stalking Code and the 2007 Model Stalking Code, state stalking laws continue to vary widely. Although state laws tend to define stalking generally as "a course of conduct directed at a specific person that would cause fear," there is little consistency in how they define specific elements of the crime.

Dr. Tjaden reviewed variations in definitions in stalking laws from one state to another. For example, she said, "course of conduct" is variously defined. Some stalking laws continue to specify what acts are included in course of conduct, and others focus on outcome — what would cause a reasonable person fear. Some statutes require visual proximity, and others recognize that with the advent of electronic monitoring and tracking technologies, stalkers don't have to maintain physical proximity to terrorize their victims. Stalking statutes also vary in the number of acts it takes to commit the crime of stalking. Though most statutes require two or more acts, some accept one act. Stalking laws also vary with respect to proxies, with some statutes specifying whether third parties can be used to stalk, and if so, who they may be.

Dr. Tjaden identified "intent" as another element that is variously defined. She noted that all stalking statutes address intent, but that they vary with respect to whether they require general intent or specific intent. Under laws with general intent, the state must prove the stalker intended the actions in which he/she engaged but does not have to prove that the stalker intended the consequences of those actions. Under laws with specific intent, the state must prove the stalker intended to cause the result of his/her actions, such as fear.

The threat requirement, Dr. Tjaden said, is another element that varies widely from statute to statute. Early stalking laws required the stalker to make a "credible threat" of violence against the victim. This threat had to be explicit, and the state had to prove the stalker was able to carry it out. Today, most state stalking laws require only an implicit threat, meaning the threat doesn't have to be conveyed in words. Usually the threat must meet a reasonable-person standard.

Fear, Dr. Tjaden added, is the fundamental justification for stalking laws: Without fear, there is no crime of stalking. Stalking statutes vary with respect to what the victim fears, such as serious bodily injury, death, sexual assault, lack of safety or substantial emotional distress. They also vary with respect to who the target of the fear is: Is it only the victim or is it also family members and acquaintances? Finally, stalking statutes vary with respect to the standard of fear or what is required regarding the victim's fear: Must the state prove the victim experienced actual fear? For example, his/her emotional state or lifestyle was altered? Or does the state need only prove that the behavior would case a reasonable person fear?

Given the wide variety of ways that states deal with these elements, Dr. Tjaden observed, it is not surprising that criminal justice practitioners are often unclear about what constitutes stalking. Without clarity in the law, she said, it is unlikely that the crime of stalking will be enforced.

Discussion of Research Gaps: Policy and Legislation

Using the discussion questions as a guide, participants were asked to discuss research gaps and critical research questions to consider as related to policy and legislation.

Enforcement of laws
- Research questions are interwoven because it is possible to have a poorly written law, but to have prosecutors and law enforcement personnel who are making the law work — and it is also possible to have a model law that is not being enforced.
- The stalking field has taken a different track than intimate partner violence, but we can learn from the intimate partner violence field, in which legislation was used against the

victims. We need to consider the reason a victim does not display fear — it could be a defense mechanism.

- The law is not inflexible, and there is room for much more creativity depending on which law is used. Different jurisdictions have different levels of monitoring ability, which relates to cost. Therefore we do not have good data on stalkers.
- It is recommended that legislation be written broadly enough to survive constitutional analysis and allow flexibility to accommodate local jurisdictional analysis.
- A new law in France seeks to criminalize psychological abuse.

Standardization

- We need standardization and clarity. In a frontier state (inhabited by 6 or fewer people per square mile), there may be differences we have not considered, and some responses in the law may not be so useful for people in these states.
- We can put a model forward, but it is up to the states to adopt it. The current model was published in 2007, and since then at least five states have moved to amend their stalking legislation with guidance from the Model Code. It would be good to see the outcomes of this change, both civil and criminal, in reporting, arrests and prosecution.
- One possible benefit of standardization would be an opportunity to conduct research because certain data elements would be central to certain types of forms. For example, protective orders now feature a standardized cover sheet that looks the same regardless of state. Forms drive practice so standardized forms might help us move toward more predictable practice.
- The Model Code has no age restriction. We are hesitant to label people younger than 18 as stalkers, and with adolescent behavior, stalking is even more contextual than among adults. The response of the victim is different, but the behavior itself is exactly the same. In general there is a dearth of research on adolescent stalking.

Technology

- Most stalking involves the use of technology, and the technology piece is an area ripe for research. For example, investigators could look at stalking through frequent texting, with messages regularly sent asking the victim where he/she is, what he/she is doing, and where he/she is going.
- GPS monitoring and surveillance of stalkers may raise privacy concerns.
- Cyber-stalking is a behavior that never starts or ends online. We should not treat cyber-stalking differently from how we treat other types of stalking. Cyber-stalking is just a tool, a specialization, another way to stalk.
- We need to avoid the term "cyber-stalking" and frame discussion around the use of technology in stalking.

Jurisdiction

- Situations are increasing in which protective orders may have expired, the offender and victim are in different states, and the victim does not know in which state to file.

- States and counties need to be able to work together to address stalking, especially since it often crosses jurisdictional boundaries.

Discussion of Research Gaps: Victim Services and Safety

Using the discussion questions as a guide, participants were asked to discuss research gaps and critical research questions to consider as related to victim services and safety.

Research
- We need to keep an open mind and not just focus on intimate partner stalking. A high rate of victimization includes stalking. We need to make sure research doesn't get too narrow.
- We need research on instances when children are used.
- There are no tools that take into account threat behavior as it relates to stalking.

Victim services
- Many communities have only a rape crisis hotline; most communities have services for victims of intimate partner violence or sexual assault; and fewer than five have dedicated services for stalking victims. We need to analyze existing practices and how they help or hurt stalking victims, e.g., some shelters refuse to accept stalking victims, and some take their cell phones when they enter. What models address stalking victims' safety, and are they effective?
- Many victims go to mental health clinics because they can't sleep, have anxiety, etc. We need to look at the mental health response, as victims will not always seek out "victim" services but may instead speak to their health care provider or therapist.
- We know a lot about victim's responses to stalking (distress). From the health literature, we see that the more severe the stalking the more likely the victim will seek help. But we do not really know how to help them. Different things seem to be effective at different times, so we need a more longitudinal perspective.
- How are needs different or similar, and how does that inform service provision?

Funding
- A challenge for service providers is that you have to develop a relationship so victims can come back repeatedly, which is hard given diminishing resources.
- In victim services, the uncertainty is resources. What would stalking victims find most useful? Real transportation alternatives? Particular economic resources? Safety measures and alarms? Legal fees, health and mental health treatment, employment compensation?
- Stalking is a different crime in terms of victims' services staff. Often there will be 40 or 50 cases but no resolution. It becomes a real funding issue. We need to influence funding.
- Help with transportation fees would be an important benefit for those having problems getting to court.

Economic costs

- Both short- and long-term economic costs of stalking must be examined so public policy can be reformed to give restitution to crime victims.
- For victims trying to escape (if only across town), affordability means being able to get excused from a lease and find affordable housing. In New York City, those options are available but are not used because other services are not in place.

Victims' resources

- Non-intimate partner victims have more resources, advice and support. With intimate partners, women are told things like, "This is how men are." Similar to what the literature shows on sexual assault, the further removed (socially) the assailant is from the victim, the more positive the response of others (supporting the "innocent victim").
- We need to investigate effective social support that would be available when needed and methods of promotion of those positive supports.

Outcomes

- How do we define success? Once success is defined, it will affect our response.
- We are looking only at victims who have sought help. Does that limit us in our approach? What about victims who are not active help-seekers?
- Results differ between victims who have a support network and those who do not. One of the hallmarks of stalking is slow isolation of the victim.

Stalking desistance

- The primary reasons for escape are reported as "I moved away," or the stalker "got another love interest."
- Denver uses the Witness Protection Program — the only service available when a victim is in imminent danger.
- How often does a stalker succeed? Maybe stalking ends because the stalker is living with the victim.

Stalking and other types of violence in specific locations

- **Workplace violence.** We might not get specific interventions in the workplace, but we may get some protection.
- **Public street stalking.** Although it is a nuisance element and not a fear element, a related issue is public space restriction, e.g., getting from your apartment to the subway without being followed or groped. This does not fit in the crime scope, but it does fit in life experience. When people have to constrain their life patterns, it constitutes stalking.

Discussion of Research Gaps: Offender Management and Offenders

Using the discussion questions as a guide, participants were asked to discuss research gaps and critical research questions to consider as related to offender management and offenders.

Reporting and prosecuting
- Cases are neither reported nor prosecuted, even though we know the behavior occurs.

Stalkers and stalking
- We need offenders' perspectives on why they stopped stalking to help us to determine if there are effective treatments for stalkers.
- Preliminary data show that risk for violence is very low in the general population, but battering is different.
- Often offenders are not convicted of stalking, but of other crimes like burglary, vandalism, etc.
- There are about a dozen typologies for stalkers, but the value of typologies needs to be further explored.
- Stalking is a dynamic risk factor. When do actions turn into stalking? Multiple regression analysis indicates that the primary predictor of stalking is the stalker's controlling behavior.
- Offenders are resourceful; many have jobs and are functional members of society.
- Stalking assessment and management assessment covers all offender variables, except victim variables. It is important to understand variations across stalking offenders especially as it pertains to their victim (e.g., intimate partner, stranger).
- It is also important to consider the extent to which stalking fits under the umbrella of controlling behavior.

Intervention
- We should do more with stalkers than intimate partner violence counseling.
- Work with probation caseloads leads to identification of stalking, which allows another 2 to 4 years to intervene with the stalker. Would educating stalkers help? Would use of various terms help in a supervision model?
- It is important to keep in mind that stalkers can get ideas for stalking methods from discussions intended to help.
- There is an effective day-release pre-trial program, and stalking and harassment offenders have a 95-percent compliance rate.
- The pre-trial period can be a crisis period or an educational period. It could encourage offenders to have some kind of pre-court education.
- We need good models of supervision. Are specialized caseloads better than non-specialized?

Immediate response
- More engagement of first responders would be good. What could we train law enforcement officers to do when they're talking to a victim?
- Maryland law enforcement officers screen on the spot, which allows the offender to be referred immediately.

GPS monitoring

- GPS only works if the offender cooperates, which leads to the importance of the case manager's relationship with the offender. We need to understand how to refer offenders to case managers when appropriate.
- Different GPS vendors also introduce problems, but we can have back-up mechanisms to ensure accountability.
- Ensure that victims don't get a false sense of security.
- GPS cannot protect victims, and a person can protect them only to the degree of the information he or she has. It is important to understand risks.

Intimate partner violence and sexual assault
- We have a good intimate partner violence program, but even the people who manage that program do not understand stalking.
- There are stalkers and non-stalkers in intimate partner violence programs. The core of intimate partner violence is control.
- Stalking often precedes or follows sexual assault.

Mental health therapy
- Lack of mental health resources leads to lack of maintenance of recovery from stalking behavior.
- Stalking harm is more psychological than physical, so risk assessment must focus on duration.

Training
- Training may be overrated, but we need to know how it is organized, how effective it is, and whether it can be modified. By interviewing prisoners, we may be able to get information on gaps in the system.

Methodology and tools
- Response tends to be principle-driven rather than protocol-driven.
- We need longitudinal research on stalking. We need to know what happens over time: late-stage abusers may be more dangerous than early-stage ones. Does abuse lead to stalking, which leads to murder?
- There is no research to demonstrate that tools to identify criminogenic factors get to the risk of stalking. We use one tool for everybody, regardless of risk, but many have static risk factors.
- Are there tools that already work?

Next Steps and Wrap-up

Participants wrote their primary concern, a critical research area or both on a piece of paper and gave it to Mr. Auchter or Ms. Backes.

Compilation of primary concerns
- Need for accurate performance measures for the criminal justice response to stalking.
- Ways in which the field can get the criminal justice system to take stalking seriously, particularly in intimate partner violence cases.
- Need for effective training for criminal justice components including corrections and parole/probation personnel.
- Assessment of training needs of criminal justice personnel as related to stalking, including the technological advances in stalking.

Compilation of critical research areas
- Research with offenders regarding what intervention(s) made them stop their stalking behavior.
- Evaluative research of programs for the prevention of primary violence against women to see if these programs actually prevent crime.
- An audit of law enforcement and prosecutorial records to examine cases of felony and misdemeanor stalking.
- Longitudinal study of stalkers to examine their patterns: Do they stalk many different victims over time?
- Qualitative research examining stalking from multiple perspectives such as the victim, offender, prosecution and law enforcement.
- Longitudinal research to explore what strategies are effective at different points in an ongoing stalking situation (for both victims and offenders).
- Research on the gaps between law enforcement responses, availability of victim services and victim cooperation in prosecution of stalking cases.
- Research to determine the factors that contribute to prosecutors' determination that a stalking case is prosecutable.
- Examination of how research methods (types of questions, stalking definitions, etc.) impact results.
- Review of efficacy of pre-trial services.
- Nexus between suicide and stalking for both victims and offenders.
- Examination of differences in treatments for victims experiencing intimate partner violence and stalking and those experiencing only stalking.
- Examination of whether the Model Code enacted in five states has made a difference.

Meeting adjourned at 4:30 p.m.

Appendix I
Agenda

8:30 a.m. to 9 a.m.	**Registration and Continental Breakfast**
9 a.m. to 9:15 a.m.	**Welcome & Opening Comments** *Kristina Rose, Acting Director, National Institute of Justice*
9:15 a.m. to 9:30 a.m.	**Facilitator Introductory Remarks & Overview** *Bernie Auchter, Acting Division Director, National Institute of Justice* *Bethany Backes, Social Science Analyst, National Institute of Justice*
9:30 a.m. to 9:45 a.m.	**Introductions**
9:45 a.m. to 10 a.m.	**Overview of Stalking Research** *T.K. Logan, Professor, University of Kentucky*
10 a.m. to 10:45 a.m.	**Discussion of Research Gaps: Law Enforcement and Prosecution** *Facilitated Discussion*
10:45 a.m. to 11 a.m.	**Break**
11 a.m. to 11:45 a.m.	**Discussion of Research Gaps: Law Enforcement and Prosecution** *Continued Facilitated Discussion*
11:45 a.m. to 1 p.m.	**Working Lunch: Presentation on the National Crime Victimization Survey: Stalking Victimization in the United States** *Katrina Baum, Senior Statistician, Bureau of Justice Statistics*
1:00 p.m. to 1:45 p.m.	**Issues with Measurement and Sampling** *Facilitated Discussion*
1:45 p.m. to 2 p.m.	**Break**

2:00 p.m. to 2:10 p.m.   **Stalking Policy and Legislative Overview**
Patricia Tjaden, Director, Tjaden Research Corporation

2:10 p.m. to 2:55 p.m.   **Discussion of Research Gaps: Policy and Legislation**
Facilitated Discussion

2:55 p.m. to 3:40 p.m.   **Discussion of Research Gaps: Victim Services and Safety**
Facilitated Discussion

3:40 p.m. to 4:20 p.m.   **Discussion of Research Gaps: Offender Management**
Facilitated Discussion

4:20 p.m. to 4:30 p.m.   **Next Steps and Wrap-up**

Discussion Questions

These questions will be used as a guide for discussion for the workshop and will be the same across all topics listed on the agenda. For each discussion area (e.g., research gaps in law enforcement and prosecution, issues with measurement and sampling), we will address each of these questions. Feel free to write down notes ahead of time for each of the agenda items, and bring your ideas to the meeting.

1. What are the current research findings regarding this topic?

2. Are there any promising practices in place regarding this topic? If so, have they been evaluated?

3. What are the research gaps for this topic?

4. Pertaining to this topic area, what do you think is the most critical research question that should be addressed in the next 5 years?

APPENDIX II: Participant List

1. Michele Archer
   Safe Horizon
   Director
   Brooklyn Criminal & Supreme Court Programs
   Anti-Stalking Program

2. Bernie Auchter
   Acting Division Director
   Violence and Victimization Research Division
   National Institute of Justice

3. Bethany Backes
   Social Science Analyst
   Violence and Victimization Research Division
   National Institute of Justice

4. Katrina Baum
   Senior Statistician
   Bureau of Justice Statistics

5. Lauren Bennett-Cattaneo
    George Mason University
    Clinical Psychology Program
    Department of Psychology

6. Amanda Cardone
    Project Coordinator
    International Association of Chiefs of Police

7. Millicent Crawford
    Victim Justice Program Specialist
    Program Development and Dissemination Division
    Office for Victims of Crime

8. Michele Galietta
    Associate Professor
    John Jay College of Criminal Justice

9. Michelle Garcia
    Director
    Stalking Resource Center
    National Center for Victims of Crime

10. Nancy Halverson
    Correctional Unit Supervisor
    Hennepin County Community Corrections

11. Barbara Hart
    Director of Law and Policy: VAWA
    Muskie School of Public Service
    University of Southern Maine

12. Andy Klein

Senior Research Analyst
Advocates for Human Potential, Inc.

13. T.K. Logan
Professor
University of Kentucky

14. Angela Moore
Acting Division Director
Justice Systems Research Division
National Institute of Justice

15. Rebecca Odor
Family Violence Program Specialist
Administration for Children and Families
Department of Health and Human Services

16. Jane Palmer
Research Assistant
Violence and Victimization Research Division
National Institute of Justice

17. Cynthia Pappas
    Senior Social Science Analyst
    Community Oriented Policing Services

18. Kristina Rose
    Acting Director
    National Institute of Justice

19. Marnie Shiels
    Attorney Advisor
    U.S. Department of Justice
    Office on Violence Against Women

20. Ben Stevenson
    Correctional Specialist III
    Department of Correction and Rehabilitation
    Pre-Trial Supervision

21. Kevin Sweeney
    Grants Program Specialist
    Office on Violence Against Women

22. Patricia Tjaden
    Director
    Tjaden Research Corporation

23. Sarah Tucker
    Technology Safety Specialist
    National Network to End Domestic Violence

www.ingramcontent.com/pod-product-compliance
Lightning Source LLC
Chambersburg PA
CBHW080755290526
45790CB00008B/3447